Congratulations!
Now What?

Bill Cosby

Congratulations!
Now What?

A Book for Graduates

HYPERION

New York

ISBN 0-7868-6572-5

Book design by Richard Oriolo

FIRST EDITION
10 9 8 7 6 5 4 3 2 1

To Mary Forchic,

who taught me in the sixth grade
with the hope that I would someday
move to the seventh.

My warm thanks to
my partner in letters,

Ralph Schoenstein.

Contents

Congratulations!
Now What?

As I Look Out at
Your Foggy Faces

Congratulations!

You have just finished four years of college and I wonder if you know what that means. It means you have lost four years in starting a real life, if you happen to be planning on one. Of course, if you had been in a Turkish prison, you might have lost even more, but you wouldn't have had to take gym.

Maybe you went to a junior college and finished in two years. However, if you went to a four-year college and paid *attention* for two, you have still…well, you get the point, which might be a new experience for you.

Or perhaps, like so many students today, you did your four years in five or six, in what could be called college interruptus. Perhaps you even lost *track* of what year you were in because you suddenly found yourself a junior with fourteen credits and the dean suggested you take another shot at getting something from the sophomore year.

Well, in whatever way you've done it, you are finally through. They may have told you that you were through in your freshman year, but you managed to hang on. It wasn't hard, of course, to hang on as a freshman because one of the school's hallowed traditions was not to give refunds right away; that first thirty thousand can buy a point guard. However, no matter what the reason, you did stay at college for the next three or four or five years, and do you know the meaning of your hanging around? You don't, so let me tell you because I have more degrees than a malaria patient.

It means you have moved from fantasy to reality. Fantasy is the life in which your parents were the search and rescue squad that saved your precious little tail again and again. Reality is knowing that your liberal arts degree will get you no job besides a restaurant receptionist.

"Welcome to the Four Seasons," you will brightly say. "Smoking or nonsmoking?"

You are well qualified for this particular career: At college, you learned what the four seasons are (as well as the days of the week); and now you can show off by reciting them in the correct order to your parents' friends. You see, your biggest job right now, the only one for which you are qualified besides taking reservations and parking cars, is to make your parents feel good by telling their friends that you entered college and managed to come out the other end.

You don't have to tell these friends precisely how long you hung out on the campus, where you spent a lot of time wondering why the cafeteria had no salad bar. You don't have to tell them that you decided to make the most of your academic opportunities by transferring from Tulane to South Sedonia Community College, where you majored in cactus. The only problem in going to an Arizona school was that you never knew when your midwinter doldrums should begin.

At South Sedonia, you also studied communications and archeology. That means you are qualified to talk to the dead.

"So, you've finally been graduated, eh?" your father's CPA will say. "With distinction?"

"No, I didn't take distinction," you'll reply. "I don't think they gave it at Purdue."

That didn't matter, of course, because you didn't go to Purdue, but rather to a college that has a good chance of one day receiving accreditation.

"Well," he will say, pretending he is interested, the same way you pretended at school, "were you at least graduated magna carta?"

"No, I was graduated Thursday."

"And now you're just weighing your options, eh?"

"Not really."

"Well, no matter what anyone has told you, your college career has still been of value. There would be no top of the class if there weren't a bottom. Did you at least have a major?"

"Oh, yes: language," you will proudly say. "Yes, I can remember it—I have a terrific memory—and it was definitely language."

"I'm afraid I don't quite understand that. Any *particular* languages?"

"Yes, I think I took Spanish and French. Or was it Italian and Greek? I know it didn't sound like English."

"And what are you going to do with your languages?"

"Gosh, I haven't given it that much thought. You know, someone told me that college is not to get you a job."

"Well, it's probably not to get *you* one. But don't take offense; not *everyone* is cut out to contribute to society, or even a blood bank."

"Absolutely. College is more than just dumping another drone into the workplace. College is a *rite of passage*. By the way, do you happen to know if that's R-I-T-E, like in Rite Aid drugs, or R-I-G-H-T, like in right kidney?"

"You certainly have an inquisitive mind, even though one of your languages isn't English. You know, with your other ones, you might be able to work at the UN."

"Does their cafeteria take reservations?"

"If not, you seem to be the kind of young man who could be quite successful stacking trays."

"My mother says I also have a flair for clearing tables. Especially when I sit down at one."

"Tell me, what was your minor?"

"My minor was film. I was especially interested in the social significance of the Three Stooges. I saw them as metaphors for what would have happened if the Three Wise Men had come to California. I did my term paper on the meaning of 'Yuk, yuk, yuk.' As a basic comment on American civilization, does 'Yuk, yuk, yuk' mean things are very funny, or 'I think I may lose my lunch'?"

"So, you're interested in film, eh? Well, I may just have a connection for you with a place that does one-hour developing."

"Is one-hour developing part of the auteur school?"

Yes, after four years of dedicating yourself to sending for pizzas while playing Tomb Raider, after four years of spending night after night at the library checking out bodies instead of books, after four years of lowering your expectations while increasing your credit lines, is there anything *else* you can do?

In the words of General Custer when he spotted five thousand Sioux: What *now*?

For these four years, you've been asking the Big Questions:

- Why doesn't this campus have HBO?
- Where is the April third *People*?
- Did Joan of Arc have dates in the army or were all the Frenchmen too short for her?

- If Shakespeare was Bacon, was Bacon anyone else?

- If the universe is fundamentally absurd, why do I need a tetanus shot?

- Will seniors have career guidance for insider trading?

And now that you have failed to answer those, you are moving on to even *Bigger Questions*:

- How early can early retirement be?

- Can my portfolio also contain a tuna fish sandwich?

- Do I register to vote at the bursar's office?

- Can an English major hope to be anything but a guide on a tourist bus?

- Can a language major hope to be anything but a guide on a tourist bus?

- Can an anthropology major hope to be anything but the driver of a tourist bus?

As you turn from the ivory tower toward the world of aluminum siding, have you hit the ground running? That's a mixed metaphor, of course, something you would know if you hadn't cut English for the month of October. But what was the point of taking something you already, like, speaked?

Well, today, you finally hold your degree. If it's a BA, you have letters that proudly stand for Barely Able because you are now someone who:

- Thinks withholding tax means not paying taxes.
- Thinks a debenture is made by an orthodontist.
- Thinks a bar code is drinking rules.
- Thinks that collateral is a quarterback's move.
- Always makes sure to tip the full ten percent.
- Thinks an index fund is a fund that lists all the other funds alphabetically.

- Thinks that HMO plays SMU.
- Thinks the electoral college is a school with no required courses.
- Thinks that parental sex is an oxymoron.
- Or is an oxymoron a moron who went to Oxford?

And one more big question: Why did you *go* to college? Because you were finally pushed out of high school and found yourself with four free years? Yes, that certainly was a basic part of your motivation. However, you also went because your parents kept saying to you, "There is nothing more important than a college degree. Without it, you will end up playing the saxophone in a bus station. No, that's not true. Playing a saxophone in a bus station calls for talent. Without it, you'll be sweeping up there."

And so, I passed on this message to my own children: Even if you become a rap singer, get your degree first. I was lying, of course; that's what parents do best. They know very well that Puff Daddy didn't need 120 credits. And they know that many famous people never got a college degree, people like Thomas Alva Edison, Harry S. Truman, and John Wilkes Booth.

However, college *was* a wonderful time —except, of course, when it was trying to teach you things; but it's just as well that you ignored those things because they didn't really prepare you for life. College is wonderful because it has nothing to *do* with life. College is not a microcosm of the world, whether or not you know what a microcosm is. (Even if you think a microcosm calls for antibiotics, it won't affect your chance to start a career in raking leaves.) The total lack of connection between college and the world is why a big man on campus is often never heard from again, except when he hands out his resumé at reunions. If you plan to do any peaking in life, don't do it at college, where it doesn't count.

Oh, you don't recall peaking at college? Good. It still may be downhill for you from now on, but it won't be such a steep slope.

What college basically prepares you for is calls from the alumni fund asking if you would like to help the school put up a new building named for an alumnus who laundered an impressive amount of money for the school.

"Hi, is this Rick Rancid?"

"Let me check my wallet and see."

"Ah, you haven't lost that old Terminal State sense of humor."

"Yes, I thought the school was pretty funny, but I couldn't get into a real one."

"You're rolling, Rick, so how about helping us get rolling with a pledge to the alumni fund for old TS? We'd love to replace some of those buildings that the kids have destroyed."

"Okay, put me down for three-fifty."

"Three-fifty! Wonderful!"

"I'd give a full five bucks, but I don't get my allowance until I start making my bed."

"Rick, you're a Terminal Stater, all right, mauve and magenta through and through. By the way, I hope I'm not disturbing you."

"Oh, no; three A.M. is when I like to take calls from the school. It's when I used to begin my assignments—that is, if I ever felt like doing one."

College also prepares you for the ability to eat the kind of food that must have been what one of the noted Western thinkers—it was either Nietzsche or Gerald Ford—had in mind when he said, "Whatever doesn't kill me, makes me stronger."

Your parents encouraged you to eat the food in the dining hall because they wanted you to feel a part of the college, because they wanted you to be fed regularly, and because they had paid for it. Therefore, college did give you one valuable thing: an immunity to ptomaine.

What college *didn't* teach you is how to rent an apartment from someone whose role model is Genghis Khan, how to shop in a market that sells more than Tic Tacs and beer, and how to work for a boss who may be evolution's missing link. You may know the formula for pi, but you probably don't know that food can actually be cooked, that no job except working as a hit man will let you create your own schedule, and that the "float" is not drifting in a pool but the way that banks make money during the week that you think a check has cleared.

You *might* be able to learn supermarket prices —just multiply the value of an item times three—but banks will forever be incomprehensible. You learned in history class that there was a depression in Prussia in 1603 (a *lot* of people were depressed in Prussia then, and the rest of the time too), but you don't know that a bank will charge you an extra dollar to use its ATM machine because, as one bank president movingly said, "We have the cost of maintaining those machines."

Really, Mister President? Then why haven't the banks been charging people for the maintenance of the *tellers*, who need more than a dollar's worth of coffee, doughnuts, and paper towels every day? You also don't know that a bank will charge *you* for money wired to your account by someone who has already been charged by *his* bank for sending the money, although the bank does waive any charge for the manager's lunch.

In short, you leave college not knowing that banks should give their presidents medical plans that cover exorcisms too.

These and many other grim truths are the cold shower of life that is about to rain on someone who has just spent four years wondering if reality exists outside the mind. When you get your first call from a collection agency, you will proudly flaunt your new knowledge and say, "But I'm afraid you don't understand: A debt is merely your subjective *idea* of indebtedness projected to an existential reality."

"You'll be hearing from our lawyer," a voice will say. "His specialty is existential reality."

"But if a lawyer is talking and I'm not listening, does he make any sound? You know, Santayana said—"

"Is Santayana *your* lawyer? Is he licensed to practice outside Cuba?"

"He represents *humanity*."

"Then he has too many cases to find time for yours and you'll be losing your credit rating."

"As long as I'm a credit to the human race."

"This office doesn't know anything about the human race. That's a different department."

You went to college because your parents had convinced you that it was a necessary step toward your future. For *me*, however, college was my second choice. My first choice was to go to Rio and find the woman in *Black Orpheus*, but I only had the money to reach Atlantic City. And I got some financial aid from college, but none was being offered by Rio.

I went to Temple, just after the end of the Ice Age, when the morning routine for a student was very different from what it is now. What high-tech merriness that routine is today! After a quick game of Bond on her PC, the student goes skateboarding to class, which is probably an elective in urban studies called Columbus: The Man and the Circle. But no matter what class she skates into, her mind is sharply focused: She takes her seat and gives her full attention to her beeper because she is expecting a call from her electrologist. Not every student has a beeper, of course. Some simply leave their cell phones on.

"A classroom today is like an annex of AT&T," one professor told me. "And the students keep putting me on hold."

For whom the bell tolls? It's call waiting.

When I was at Temple, I had one elderly professor who passed me on the campus one afternoon for the second time that day.

"Mr. Crosley," he said, almost remembering me, "did you happen to pass me earlier today?"

"Yes, sir," I replied. "About one o'clock."

"And was I going in *this* direction?"

"You were."

"Oh, good! That means I had lunch."

Now that man had a brilliant mind, but it didn't happen to be in this particular universe. I'm sure you had teachers like that too, people who were fine to guide you through the soul but who weren't the ideal guides for fighting with the company that was pretending to give you automotive insurance.

"What do you *mean* 'five hundred dollars deductible'?" you will say. "The repair only cost me four-fifty."

"Then you owe us only fifty dollars," a voice will graciously reply. "And I'm happy to tell you that there's a grace period for your premium increase. It won't take effect for another forty-eight hours."

"*Premium* increase? The other driver hit *me*! I was the *victim*!"

"Please don't get hysterical, Mr. Crosby. *All* of us are victims in one way or another, aren't we? Why, I remember when my own mother…"

At Temple, I majored in phys ed because I liked a class with no books, a class where the homework was push-ups, and I never wondered what the liberal arts were preparing me for because I didn't know the liberal arts from the martial arts.

Well, many of you graduates who are now setting forth on a great adventure in floundering also gave little thought to whether you'd be prepared for it. When you arrived at the school four years ago, you probably heard the dean say something like this:

"I want to welcome you freshmen to Terminal State College. I'm delighted that all of you chose this as your safety school. Terminal State is a liberal arts college that puts no particular emphasis on varsity sports, as you can tell from the scores.

"Four years from now, it will be my pleasure to give a few of you liberal arts degrees. But what does a liberal arts degree *mean* in our fast-buck world? Will the study of Dante, whoever he may be, help to get you a job at Microsoft? Will Shakespeare place you in General Motors? Only if he's a vice president there. No, after four years here, you won't know how to fix a car or build a septic tank or do any one useful thing. You will leave this school as unprepared as you have entered it, and maybe with a new tattoo. But two or three of you may know how to think."

And those two or three will be able to spell all the words on their applications for unemployment insurance. They won't *get* unemployment insurance, of course, because there must be work that they are *out* of and they decided to learn Keats instead of refrigeration. Since 1980, more than 43 million jobs have been erased in the United States; but you probably wouldn't have gotten one anyway.

What about starting your own business and working for yourself? Well, let me ask you: Would *you* give a job to someone like you?

The best thing for you is to take the long view and start planning for your retirement, even if it is hard to distinguish from your professional life. A recent survey of college students found that 64 percent of them believe that they will retire before the age of fifty. Why not get a good jump on it?

I know it's too late to tell you this as you try to stop yourself from thinking <u>Now</u> what?, but when you started school and heard that speech from the dean, you should have transferred to Midas Muffler A&M. A lot of your fellow students spent four years thinking and what they mostly thought about was how long they could live with their parents before the parents sneaked off to Venezuela.

"College didn't really teach me how to think," one graduate told me. "Just what to think."

"And what *did* you think about?" I asked him.

"How nice it was that I found a date for the prom in the student rehab center. She looked so lovely drying out."

"Liquor was a problem at your school?"

"No, it was easy to get. Unless, of course, you forgot and used your real ID."

Because most graduates have just spent four years primarily preparing to receive the alumni magazine, I try to keep pointing the way for them at commencements, an ironic word for people who may be commencing nothing more than a life at Blockbuster Video. In fact, giving commencement speeches is a hobby of mine; I have a feeling for anesthesiology. Moreover, I like to give young people a chance to hear the important ideas they plan to ignore.

"Mr. Cosby, I hear you made a wonderful talk today," a Spelman graduate told me right after a commencement she had been partially in.

"Thank you," I told her. "I wish you could have heard it. Too bad you didn't set your alarm."

"Would you mind taking a moment to sum it up for me?"

"Of course not. What I basically said was Plato's classic advice: Be out of your room by Friday."

No matter how many of the graduates are unconscious at commencement, I always like to tell them such inspirational things. I also like to quote from Aristotle and say, "Get a job." Don't take the next ten or fifteen years trying to find yourself. You will always be right there, trying to get out of bed while wondering if you're qualified for a career as a crossing guard.

Since you'll be ignoring my advice, you are probably telling people that you now want to take a few years off to find yourself. Well, I'm from a different generation. When I was in college, I never tried to find myself, no matter how many people kept telling me to get lost.

Chapter Two

Your Future May
Be Behind You

All right, let's get specific about your future, which may or may not have begun. All across America right now, the following scene is being played. If you haven't yet been part of it, you probably will, unless you enter the witness protection program to keep your parents from bothering you.

FATHER OF GRADUATE: What a wonderful day!

GRADUATE: Which one?

FATHER: *This* one.

GRADUATE: Some reason why?

FATHER: You finally have your *degree*.

GRADUATE: Yes, I have it somewhere. I think it's in Harry's room. Unless I left it on the subway. But don't worry, Dad, my name is on it and I'm sure someone in the subway system reads Latin.

FATHER: I don't care about any lost and found. For the first time in your life, I'm *proud* of you.

GRADUATE: Yes, wasn't it great the way I remembered to return all those library books? That certainly helped me graduate.

FATHER: Frankly, my boy, I wasn't sure that you knew where the library was.

GRADUATE: Oh, I certainly did. I found it right at the start of my sophomore year. You couldn't have a library date unless you found the library.

FATHER: You know, that library has more than two million books.

GRADUATE: Yes, I almost read one.

FATHER: Son, it's time to look ahead.

GRADUATE: Any special reason why?

FATHER: That's what your graduation speaker said.

GRADUATE: No, I think he said, "It's time to book a bed." But I could be wrong. I usually was on the tests.

FATHER: Well, it's time to talk about your future. I'm afraid you see it as another elective.

GRADUATE: It *isn't?*

FATHER: I'm afraid not. Son, have you thought about a job?

GRADUATE: I like the way you call me "son."

FATHER: Well, there's a good chance that you are. So what about a job?

GRADUATE: For whom? Notice the way I said that: for *whom.* I plan to be speaking a lot of English now.

FATHER: A job for *you.* Or is it for *youm?*

GRADUATE: Well, my expectations are quite high, so I'm not going to jump into just anything.

FATHER: I hear there's an opening at the car wash.

GRADUATE: Okay, I'll send them my resumé. Does being a lifeguard count?

FATHER: At the car wash, it might. I just hope they're looking for geology majors.

GRADUATE: You think it's an entry level position?

FATHER: Yes, it's at the front of the car wash. You don't have enough experience to be a buffer.

GRADUATE: Maybe I could be an intern there.

FATHER: Last summer, weren't you an intern at the Burger King?

GRADUATE: For a while, but they let me go, even though I finally did learn what a Whopper is.

FATHER: Burger King might have been a reach for you then; but now that you're a college graduate, you've got to aim high again.

GRADUATE: Dad, I really don't want you to pressure me. I had enough of that at college getting to those ten o'clock classes. I want you and Mom to realize that I *may* be a late bloomer.

Like Grandma Moses, Winston Churchill, and Uncle Harry.

FATHER: Uncle Harry hasn't worked in forty-five years.

GRADUATE: Because *he's* selective too. The only job that really appealed to him was Secretary of State, but he just didn't get the breaks.

FATHER: Harry didn't have the advantage of going to college. If he *had* gotten a college degree, he might have been running U.S. Steel instead of numbers. Your mother and I want you to take *advantage* of your degree like other people in the family. Just look at your cousins: One is an accountant and one an engineer.

GRADUATE: Both mental cases.

FATHER: Yes, but in those twisted minds, what knowledge. Well, son, I want you to know this: No matter how many decades it takes you to get going, this will always be your home.

GRADUATE: That's beautiful, Dad.

FATHER: Just remember that your rent doesn't include utilities.

GRADUATE: And Dad, now I want *you* to know something: I would like to be on my own.

FATHER: *That's* what I like to hear.

GRADUATE: So can you lend me the rent?

FATHER: Of course I can. At the same twelve percent I'm paying on your college loans.

GRADUATE: How much do you owe now, Dad?

FATHER: Just two hundred eighty thousand dollars. But your mother and I are happy to owe it so you can be such an intelligent waiter.

Mention of the college loans forces me to point out that the father lied when he said, "This will always be your home" because he is deep in a chapter that you never read at school: Chapter Eleven. Your senior year cost nearly thirty thousand dollars because you selfishly insisted on having meals—and this figure doesn't include the nine hundred calls that you charged to him and the ten days you took in Fort Lauderdale because you needed a change of pace. A *genuine* change of pace for you would have been to do some assignments.

Your father, however, does have a good feeling about his destitution because *his* father didn't have the privilege of going into bankruptcy for *him*. For both your parents, no matter how homeless, you are an investment. You are bread on the water or water over the dam or some metaphor that you should have learned at college when you were busy with cybersex.

And so, your parents are about to re-create your old room in Motel Six, where they will be moving after selling the house to repay what they borrowed for you to "meet the bright tomorrow." The graduates may be dim, but tomorrow is always bright.

A friend of mine has a daughter in an Ivy League college that shall be nameless. When the daughter's senior year began, my friend got a letter from the president of Cornell (I didn't say how *long* it would be nameless) that began:

> *Dear Cornell Parent:*
> *I have good news for you. This year, the increase in the college tuition is the smallest in Cornell's history.*

Now *that* definition of good news gets an A in creative writing. I wonder if the president would like to receive a letter that began:

Dear Patient:
I have good news for you. Your X ray shows a problem, but we're offering a special on eight-by-ten glossies.

Even the top federal officials have never understood the financing of a college education. When Ronald Reagan was President, his secretary of the treasury was a man named Donald T. Regan, who was taking government pass-fail. One memorable day, Mr. Regan said, "There's too much whining about paying for college. Whatever happened to the old-fashioned idea of working your way through college?"

Well, whatever happened to the old-fashioned idea of a public official making sense? Yes, a student can certainly work his way through college today, but only if he has the Viagra concession in the faculty lounge.

College, however, does train a student to meet whatever financial pressures real life may throw at him. It is excellent early training in survival. Remember when you went to your grandmother, gave her a warm hug, and said, "Grandma, the rest of them may be thinking about your will, but not *me*; I need it right *now*, or certainly by Thursday. The bursar's office won't wait until your arteries break down. The advances in medicine are killing *me*."

Because your grandmother thoughtlessly insisted on staying alive, you learned about finance from watching your parents raise the money either by selling the house or with a financial plan like this:

> Guaranteed student loan at 12 percent interest—$5,000
>
> Guaranteed loan from heavy-set gentleman on the corner at 200 percent interest—$5,000
>
> Sale of blood at $25 a pint—$100
>
> Insurance settlement for deliberately stepping

in front of brother-in-law's car—$3,000

Second mortgage—$10,000

Third mortgage (Bank of Bolivia)—$10,000, but half in pesos

Sale of all but kitchen furniture—$4,000

However, in spite of your parents now being people that the Sioux would call Dances with Debt, they still think that you are worth their loss of a credit rating (they don't know you that well) and they are warmed by the thought that you did drop in to class from time to time, you diligently read almost all your *Cliffs Notes*, and you now have a chance to become the best educated bagger at the A&P.

"Meet the bright tomorrow."

Isn't that what the commencement speaker said? Or was it "Eat light tomorrow? Neat fight tomorrow? Meat night tomorrow?" Even *he* can't remember. You see, he came just for an honorary degree so he can call himself "doctor" and get a reservation in an exclusive restaurant.

At one commencement, I told the graduates, "Get to know the custodian where you work. He knows everything that's going on."

Unfortunately, one of the things he knows is that the only job you're fit for is his and he has it, so you may have trouble getting to know him. Advice like this from commencement speakers is the reason why it might be all right to replace them with scat singers.

But let's forget about the speaker and your parents—*you* certainly have—and focus on whether anything at all is ahead for you, except perhaps taking sacred vows and moving to Tibet. The problem is you don't know if you have had the right shots for Tibet because you left your college medical record at a Taco Bell.

There may be some guidance for you in a talk I had with my daughter when she had finished four years of college.

"Dad," she said, "I've decided that I'm ready to make a living."

"I'm truly moved to hear it," I replied, "but you may have a problem."

"Be careful, Dad. I can be easily discouraged."

"Well, I do have to be honest and tell you that you still haven't shown that you know how to clean up your room. You were away for four years and you still have a junior high school room. Did Socrates have half-eaten hoagies in his bed? Did Spinoza have a collection of dust balls? Did Kierkegaard change his sheets once a year?"

"Dad, I can't believe you! Well, I just happen to know a person who actually got a job and *she* doesn't have to clean up the office. People come in after work to do that. You know, I didn't take cleaning at college; I wasn't a sanitation major."

"That's true: The one who went to the cleaners was me. All right, if you want to move out and support yourself, let's look at the job you're going to get. First of all, you must realize that you're not qualified to do anything."

"Dad, does that really matter?"

"True, a lot of jobs need no qualifications: paving the streets, running networks, serving in the Senate…. Okay, your major was sociology."

"Right. So I'll certainly be able to be social."

"And your whole curriculum was liberal arts, so you can read and write a few sentences."

"Right. Didn't I e-mail you all the time?"

"Well, your job may be more than writing requests for money."

"I also studied the great philosophers."

"Which ones?"

"I can't remember them now, but believe me, they were great."

"And what did they teach you that can help you get a job?"

"Well…let's see…. There was this one German guy. I think it was Eisenhower."

"You mean Schopenhauer?"

"Whatever. Well, he said some wonderful words of guidance for me: He said that things never work out, so what's the point?"

"A useful approach to a job interview. Tell the interviewer that you'll show up but don't expect much because you're a pessimist."

"Right, a pessimist: someone who doesn't believe in violence."

"You know, Gandhi also didn't believe in violence and *he* cleaned up his room. And he always wore a clean sheet."

"Gandhi looked like he ate the food at our school. And Dad, there was some other philosopher —I think it was Santa Anna—who said life is a dream."

"Another excellent approach to a job," I said. "Tell the interviewer you're not sure that the company really exists."

"Dad, that's the liberal arts."

"Which prepares you to *teach* the liberal arts to other people who also won't be able to get jobs. You'll tell them, 'Life stinks; pass it on,' or 'Life is a dream; tell the others.'"

"Dad, now *I've* got to be honest: I can't look for a job right now because college left me burned out. Before I even *think* about a job, I want to take a year off."

"But you *took* a year off. When you were in college."

"Well, even when I was *going*…Dad, you've obviously forgotten what college was like."

"Of course; your schedule was much tougher than any job. Let's see…you had three or four hours of classes from Monday to Thursday and on Friday no classes at all."

"Well, aren't there any jobs that have Friday off?"

"I believe some goat herders take Friday off."

"Do they have a good medical plan?"

"So four years of that routine left you burned out, eh?"

"Well, I also had to read all those *books* and listen to all that *lecturing*."

"But they let you use a *tape* recorder, which would've gotten *me* thrown out of class."

"You've got to make sure the batteries are fresh and the sound is picking up and—"

"Okay, that's one job: You could be a spy."

"What time do spies have to get up?"

"Well, they're shot at sunrise."

"Oh, I couldn't make that."

"I'm relieved to hear it."

"And *another* thing: the *tests* at school were confusing."

"You couldn't tell what subject they were covering?"

"No, I could figure that out, but the *marking* was confusing. Take the midterm."

"Did *you* take it?"

"Yes, but my heart wasn't in it because it only counted for thirty percent of my grade, so there was no point in doing real well."

"I'm starting to understand. And that's what scares me."

"The final was seventy percent; and then another ten percent for the term paper."

"That's a hundred and ten percent."

"Dad, please don't be picky; you're a bigger man than that. Anyway, I figured I'd get an A."

"And you got?"

"A C, which isn't that *far* from an A."

"Right; it's in the same alphabet. So what happened?"

"I told you: I got burned out. That's why I'm not sure I'll be ready for a job for a few years."

"But weren't you able to study on nights and weekends?"

"I was certainly *planning* to; but on a couple of weekends, I had to help friends move because they didn't like their roommates."

"That's good training for marriage."

"And a couple of other weekends, I was really stressed because friends dropped out."

"But the ones who dropped out still liked their roommates, right? I mean, they just dropped out because they couldn't stand the pressure of going to classes four days in a row?"

"Dad, please pay attention so you'll understand the burning out."

"You know, when Mom and I asked you how you were doing, you always said, 'Fine.'"

"College kids *have* to say 'Fine.' Even that boy who dropped out to join the Gambino family said 'Fine.' You see, you and Mom wouldn't understand all these problems because they don't come up in real life. This is a different time now."

"Right; the Twilight Zone."

"A lot of the kids were doing drugs and I had to help them."

"Teach them how?"

"Dad, *please*. And a lot of the kids drank too much and I had to help them too. Three other girls, their parents were getting divorced. And I had to talk my friend Sally out of joining the Salvation Army."

"If you were working as a psychologist, why didn't you switch your major to that?"

"Dad, when you speak at all those graduations, I hope you don't say things like that."

"No, it's too late to change your major then."

"And another thing: Nobody ever came to see me."

"Your *mother and I* came and you were too busy to see us."

"You have all those degrees and you don't know the *reason*?"

"I don't have one in abnormal psychology."

"Well, frankly, I felt you were spying on me."

"Ah, the spying again. Yes, the CIA is definitely your one possibility."

"And Dad, there's one other thing. I never really liked that school."

"You have to be kidding. Honey, that school was your *first choice*."

"No, Mom made me go to it."

"Okay, let's ask her."

"I wish I could talk to her now, but I'd really like to go to my room and relax for a few weeks. You people in the real world don't understand stress."

"Okay, you go to your room and see if there's anything you might like to do for the next fifty years besides work at the Betty Ford Clinic. I'll talk to Mom about this myself."

"She won't tell you the truth."

"My own wife is going to lie to me?"

"Dad, this is exactly what builds up the stress. I graduate and all I want is for people to love me for what I am."

"But honey, right now, after four years of the college Mom made you attend, four years of C's and practicing psychiatry, what *are* you?"

"Dad, I'm really getting a headache and I don't know where you're going with this. College is all behind me now and I'm trying to forget it."

"You did that pretty well as you went along."

"Well, after some time in my room, I just want to see if I can move into my own apartment and support myself."

"Your own apartment? Well, just what rent do you have in mind?"

"I'll go as high as four hundred dollars a month."

"You plan to live in a toxic waste site? Four hundred dollars is what you have to give the doormen at Christmas. If your mother and I ever put you in a place like that, you'd call nine-one-one. Honey, do you know what a studio apartment rents for in New York or Boston or Washington?"

"What's a studio?"

"If it had one less room, it would have *no* rooms. And they'd *still* get five hundred a month for it. But with that one whole room, they get about fifteen hundred. Except when they get two thousand."

"Well, my friend Mia has a job in New York that pays four hundred dollars a week and her rent on *Madison Avenue* is only nine hundred dollars a month."

"Half of which comes from her parents. Maybe her parents will also give *you* half of yours. Maybe they're Ford Foundation people. By the way, what job do you have in mind?"

"Can I get back to you on that?"

"Certainly. Meanwhile, practice saying, 'Do you want fries with that?'"

Chapter Three

Is Real Life, Like, a Required Course?

As my children entered colleges and headed for the real world, I spent a lot of time trying to prepare them for the realities of life and my grade was D minus, which should be rounded off to an F. In fact, even though I hold an Ed.D. (Exceptionally Dense Dad), I also failed at teaching them the realities of *college* life. I did pretty well, however, in explaining the law that made them attend junior high.

I remember calling one college to see if my daughter was still enrolled and I was happy to find that she was. Being enrolled was definitely a better way to learn. And I also remember clearly when one of my other daughters was finishing her freshman year and I discovered that her GPA was 1.7.

"Don't worry," I told my wife. "She probably thinks that the GPA is like the PGA: You try for the lowest score."

"She is definitely some kind of birdie," my wife replied.

However, my daughter had such a fine mind that she knew she hadn't been using it. A few days after telling me she was sorry that her grade point average was like January in Duluth, she came up with the ideal way to put her brain in gear.

"Dad," she said with a deeply studious look, "I've thought very hard about my marks and I've figured out what's wrong."

"What's wrong is you're doing badly," I replied with the insight that had gotten me a doctorate in education.

"Oh, that may be true," she said, "but I've figured out *why*. You see, I'm doing my work in my *dorm*."

"When you should be doing it at Shea Stadium?"

"Well, I could do a lot better if I had my own apartment."

"You mean a little place of your own where you wouldn't study?"

"Dad, I've got to get away from that dorm."

"All the studying there bothers you?"

"No, you see, a lot of people in that dorm want to talk about their lives and their lives are really messed up, so I have to listen to them and they sometimes don't finish till five in the morning and then it's too late to study."

Another female Freud! What a *talent* I had for raising psychologists! My house should have been designated a branch of the Menninger Clinic.

"Can't you see your patients in the afternoon?" I said. "Oprah hears all that stuff at four o'clock."

"Dad, these people need midnight therapy. I'd

really do better in my own apartment. I could get one right on the campus."

"So you'd still be in school?"

"I would."

When my daughters had lived at home, my record of saying no to them had not been impressive. In fact, I had given them just three absolute prohibitions: no drugs but Excedrin, no running off with the Rolling Stones, and no getting married on a school night. This new request seemed to fall outside my big three of discipline.

"Well," I said firmly, "okay."

"And can I also have a car?" she said.

"But your campus is four square blocks. With no valet parking."

"Dad, you just don't understand," she said, and those were the wisest words she had spoken in her entire freshman year.

"Well…I guess it would be okay," I said, but then I quickly let her know that there were definite limits. "Honey, you don't want a Swiss bank account, do you?"

"Why would I need that?" she said. "I'm not taking Swiss."

My daughter knew how to find an apartment on campus, but campus is the world of make-believe. Few college kids ever imagine the grim reality of finding an apartment after graduation, not in Mobile, Bakersfield, or East St. Louis but in places like San Francisco, Chicago, and New York.

"Jill and I just found an apartment on the East Side!" a young friend told me recently.

"You beat everyone to the obituaries," I said.

"No, everybody uses the obituaries," he said. "That's a dead end. We got the place because a classmate of mine works in a *funeral* home and he called me. It was a woman of ninety in two rent-controlled rooms on Lexington Avenue. What mixed emotions, Bill! I felt wonderful about the apartment, of course, but I must confess that I felt a little funny too."

"Because you got the apartment from a woman who'd just passed away?"

"No, because they hadn't taken the body out yet. You think it was bad taste?"

"Did you step on her?"

"Oh, of course not. You've got to show respect."

"And you didn't kill her by any chance?"

"No, but it *is* an apartment to kill for."

College classes in urban studies are fine if you want to know how to design a mall in Pittsburgh, but they don't teach you the asphalt jungle warfare that you will be waging. They don't teach you that, when you rent an apartment, the landlord will ask you for the first month's rent in advance, a month's rent as a security deposit, a credit check, a Sam's Club card, a urine sample, and a notarized statement that you have never been employed by Saddam Hussein. Saddam, by the way, would never have dealings with anyone who has dealings with a landlord.

Yes, the world outside those ivy-covered walls is crazier than anything that ever happened on campus, even their letting you in. A recent newspaper story about the guerrilla warfare for apartments in New

York said that people wanting to rent there now are actually required to produce tax returns, W-2 forms, credit reports, letters of reference from employers, and sometimes even letters of reference about *pets!* Graduate, you've come into a world where someone wanting an apartment may have to present:

Dear Landlord:

I have known Mr. Fat Albert's cocker spaniel, Citronella, for three years and I assure you that she is free from fleas and has never given rabies to anyone or even put an innocuous hole in a mailman's leg.

She is gentle, loyal, thrifty, and of the highest character, the kind of tenant you would like to have sniffing around your building. Furthermore, she does not play loud music late at night, she does not bark at doormen, and she has borne no children by any other species.

In addition to the family values she possesses, Citronella is considerably more intelligent than Mr. Fat Albert and will be happy to countersign the lease.

A college graduate trying to settle in a big city is an asphalt innocent.

"Any apartment seems great when you first move in," one young man told me. "But six months later, there's the first shoot-out and things just don't feel the same. I tell my mother that the SWAT teams keep coming to protect me."

"The first time I came into my new building," a young woman said, "the security guy at the desk downstairs asked me who I was. And you know what I did? I showed him my Baylor ID."

"Did he let you drop any courses?" I asked her.

Speaking of landlords, bankers, and SWAT teams makes me realize that there *is* one career for which many graduates *are* prepared: white-collar crime. I have studied this syndrome in my own family. When it was her time to go to college, one of the brightest children in our family came to me and said, "Dad, here's the thing about college: I don't want to go."

"I see," I said. "In other words, you want to prepare for life by staying on the phone in your room. That's good training for a stock swindler, of course; but does there happen to be a reason why you want to cancel your future by not going to college?"

"Of *course*," she said. "I don't test well."

She was making that up, of course. Ironically, she was about to test *me*.

"So, I have a wonderful idea," she said, and I knew at once it was going to be an idea almost as good as Napoleon's invasion of Russia. "I have figured out how much you and Mom would have spent on college for me. And so, to make it easy for you, you don't have to bother to send the money there."

"That's very thoughtful of you, dear."

"You can simply give it to me in a lump sum."

"In small unmarked bills?"

"Dad, please be serious. Now the thing is, I know you may not like this idea."

"Let me think about it for a moment. You're right, I don't."

"I anticipated that, so I have an easy-pay plan: If

you'd rather, you can give me the money in install-ments."

"You want to give me a coupon book, like a loan company?"

"Oh no, Dad, I trust you. Just give me twenty-five thousand dollars a year for four years and it'll work out fine. By then, I'll have figured out what I want to do."

"I think you know right now," I said. "You'd like to be an extortionist."

Because my Temple education had made me so smart, I was able to look far ahead: If I had accepted her terms, she would have come to me after four years in her room and said, "And now, Dad, I am finished not going to college and I would like not to go to *law* school, probably Harvard."

"A wonderful school not to go to."

"I thought you'd agree. So that's seventy-five thousand for another three years. And won't it be good that I won't have all that *pressure*?"

I didn't know how good it would have been because again I was looking ahead: In another three years, she'd be saying, "Dad, by now I would have graduated fifth in my class."

"Only six people in your class?" I would say.

"And I'm ready for a *grant*. But I want to be fair, so you tell *me* what a grant for a year's study would be. In Paris."

Chapter Four

And F. Scott Fitzgerald Is the Father of Ella

Even if you are a graduate who doesn't test or dress or spell well, even if you think that La Paz is in France, syntax is a Japanese camera, the Mindanao Deep is a tango, and the heart of the Confederacy was Albania, there is still hope for you to rise in the world of business because today ability often counts least of all. If American companies were always run by smart people, would we have ever been given the

Edsel, the New Coke, 3Com Park, and the playoffs in the National Hockey League? Never, in fact, has incompetence bloomed as it is blooming in this country today, a flowering that should inspire you.

You have heard of the Peter Principle: Ineptitude, like gas, keeps rising. Well, that principle belonged to a time when American business had a better class of incompetents. Things aren't that good anymore.

Merely by *going* to college, even if your mind stayed in neutral there, you are qualified to become part of that sterling collection of the mentally handicapped known as the old boy network. For you women, of course, it is the old girl network. The problem is, however, that women are smarter than men, so the old girl network is stained by competence and harder for an airhead to crack. Most of the people who've worked on my television shows are women; they are a higher species than men.

The pioneer old boy network was formed at Princeton University to help its graduates do more than lawns. The graduate simply presents himself to a member of the network who is high in a company and either gives the secret handshake, a high five, or the wave. The only other qualification for being hired is to be free of scurvy. In this way, Princeton alumni have found employment for graduates who otherwise might have had to join the executive training programs in copper mines.

And so, even if you can't find your diploma, get a copy of the alumni directory, find a graduate in some profession that won't demand too much of you, and give him a call, which he will return after his handball game. Princeton has the *best* old boy network; it has produced executives who should be playing with clay; but every school has an old boy network, full of alumni who have read nothing but train schedules for twenty years. And since your computer skills are certainly better than theirs, the moment they place you, go for *their* jobs.

In fact, your computer skills are so overwhelming that they have replaced everything else in your head. I know a recent college graduate whose computer suddenly failed when she was trying to fill out a job application that was due the following day; and she was forced to borrow a manual portable typewriter from a friend of mine. However, moments after she got it, she called my friend and said, "You forgot to give me part of the typewriter."

"Which part?" said my friend.

"The electric cord," the young woman said.

"But there *isn't* one."

"Then how do you give it power?"

"Hand power."

"*Hand* power? I don't understand."

"You operate it…well, the same way the Egyptians built the pyramids."

"No kidding. The Egyptians had Smith-Coronas? But they didn't need surge protectors, right?"

"No, not unless the crowds really got out of hand."

This young woman had come from a world where so much of life was online that most conferences with professors were being done with e-mail and some exams were being given online, where the library was entirely the Internet and most students never traveled without their laptops, where the words "I'm having trouble at the terminal" could never have meant "I can't find my bus."

In talking about networking, perhaps I was a bit too simplistic in telling you to just get an alumni directory and call an alumnus about a job. When I mentioned this technique to one recent graduate, she said, "Well, it's really hard to make that kind of call just because the man or woman threw up on your campus twenty years ago. You're still calling a stranger who must be pretty tired of hearing from thousands of pushy kids with no credentials. So many *people* went to the school. It's like calling someone and saying, 'Hey, I'm Presbyterian too, so give me a job.'"

When I thought about what she had said, I realized that the Princeton system for mediocrity placement is probably unusual, that a more common exchange would be something like:

RECENT GRADUATE: Hello, Mr. Newton Beatty?

ANCIENT GRADUATE: Yes, this is Beatty. Are you the

Miss Feldman from the District Attorney's office?

RECENT GRADUATE: No, this is Maria *Fedderman*, Columbia '98. Remember Butler Library?

ANCIENT GRADUATE: Yes, what about it?

RECENT GRADUATE: Well, I remember it too. Ever take a book and forget to return it?

ANCIENT GRADUATE: Absolutely not. Look, how did this call—

RECENT GRADUATE: And remember old Van Am Quad?

ANCIENT GRADUATE: I also remember that I have to fire my assistant.

RECENT GRADUATE: Before you do, want to reminisce about Van Am Quad?

ANCIENT GRADUATE: A pretty ordinary place.

RECENT GRADUATE: My memories exactly; I preferred the Newark waterfront. But hey, Mr. Beatty, how about those Lions?

ANCIENT GRADUATE: The Detroit Lions? What about them?

RECENT GRADUATE: No, the Columbia Lions.

ANCIENT GRADUATE: They should be playing nuns.

RECENT GRADUATE: They'd lose. So can you give me a job?

If that scene was discouraging, do not despair: I have another bit of encouragement for you. The great trend in American business today is to fire competent older executives and replace them with college graduates who either will or won't learn on the job for about a quarter of the executive's salary. American companies are drifting toward having directors on Dermasil, a condition that already exists in the worlds of television and film. Neil Simon stopped writing movies because, as he said, "I got tired of meetings with teenagers."

And so, you may be entering a world in which your boss isn't sure of the difference between Richie Cunningham and Richard III. (He knows *one* of

them had lousy posture.) However, he won't be igno-
rant of how much he has saved by firing someone
who *does* know the difference and hiring you for what
is the minimum wage in Taiwan.

The moment you take any job, update your
resumé because the company may soon be trading
you for a mailroom worker and two custodians to be
named later. In the memorable words of former
Secretary of Labor Robert Reich, "Loyalty is dead."
They are words that one day soon may be added to
the Boy Scout oath.

As you approach the job market where these
wonderful people are waiting for you, let us review
your skills. It won't take long.

First, you know a little English. Like, hopefully.
And it is probable that you will be interviewed by
someone for whom English is also a second language.

At a midwestern campus one day, I happened to over-
hear the development of the language you will be using.

"Like, do you love her?" said one student to
another.

And the other replied, "Well, not *love*. It's like I *like* her."

I was in awe: In "Like I like her," *fifty percent* of the sentence is *like*, topping "I like Ike," which was only thirty-three percent. It made *The Philosophy of Fat Albert* sound like Sophocles. "Hey, hey, hey" is Shakespearean today.

So, you see, you went to college to learn a few things to put between the likes.

"What was your mark on the Spanish exam?" I asked my oldest daughter during her junior year.

"Like a B," she replied.

"Like a B?" I said. "What is a synonym for a B? Synonyms for letters are really hard to find."

"Dad, this is exactly why my generation doesn't like talking to yours."

"Because we use English?"

"It's showing off. Just remember: Not all of us *majored* in English."

Okay, now your *second* skill...will you settle for *one*? No, to be fair, every graduate today does have a skill that his parents lack: He may be an airhead, but he does fly through cyberspace. In fact, perhaps the most typical postgraduate conversation in America today is one like this:

PARENT: What were you saying about getting a job in pottery?

GRADUATE: No, I said I'm planning on winning the *lottery*.

PARENT: And *that's* your career plan?

GRADUATE: Do you realize how much money that is? I might even be able to move out of the house.

PARENT: That's a moving thought.

GRADUATE: Frankly, I've been living here just to spare you the heartbreak of an empty nest.

PARENT: Well, that's a stress test I'd be happy to take. But tell me: While you're waiting to win the lottery, is there *any* other job you might like to try?

GRADUATE: Well, the best jobs in America are all at computer companies. For computer support specialists, softwear development managers, database managers, wireless engineers, computer-systems analysts, and architects.

PARENT: You studied some of that?

GRADUATE: No, I just worked on memorizing the list. But in my own way, I *have* gone deeply into computers.

PARENT: You mean you've spent the last ten years playing Minesweeper?

GRADUATE: Of course not. I also played Tenchu, Mortal Kombat, Street Fighter, Metal Gear Solid, and Solitaire—sometimes half the night. Listen, do you think all that was *fun*?

PARENT: And staying up the other half of the night sending instant messages to women.

GRADUATE: The only hope for mankind is to communicate with one another.

PARENT: Sex with strangers is your way to win the Nobel Peace Prize?

GRADUATE: This is exactly why more communication is needed.

PARENT: Well, is there anything *else* that you might like to do with computers?

GRADUATE: Yes, I'd like to be a part-time air traffic controller.

PARENT: But you have absolutely no *qualifications* for that.

GRADUATE: You've never heard of on-the-job training? Anyway, I do have qualifications: You *know* I've always liked to play with planes. And wasn't I a seventh grade crossing guard? So now I'll be a crossing guard in the sky. I wonder if the airport gives armbands.

PARENT: But what about your *concentration* span?

GRADUATE: My what?

PARENT: Your concentration span.

GRADUATE: I forgot the question.

PARENT: Your *concentration* span.

GRADUATE: Well, what about it?

PARENT: You don't *have* one.

GRADUATE: I'll handle short flights.

Chapter Five

Can My Resumé be About *Moby Dick*?

Even if you happen to have a concentration span, and even if you speak a little English, and even if you let the computer company know that you'll accept a salary in yen, you still will need a resumé and it may be one that enriches American literature, for the resumés of college graduates are the reason that short fiction is having a boom in America.

Of course, the mass production of this fiction is

understandable. How do you write a resumé when you haven't done more than succeed in achieving a zip code? At least, you don't have to put down all the things that you *don't* know, like how to buy food, cook it, and help someone stop choking on it. To a college graduate, the Heimlich maneuver took place during the Battle of Tannenberg.

Because almost everything you put in your resumé will be either trivial, irrelevant, or untrue (a good resumé blends all three), the challenge to you is a big one: You have to find a mixture of lyrical lying and fanciful fraud that will impress the interviewer. As I have said, you will have one thing going for you: The company is eager to fire all those people in their late fifties who actually know something and replace them with bargain basement blanks like you.

Okay, let's get specific because the point of this book is to help you, not depress you. You'll be depressed enough at the interview.

You certainly can list a few fictitious people you've worked for, but be subtle about it. Don't say you spent a summer as a deck hand with Admiral

Byrd. Don't say you were an intern at the Bailey Building and Loan. And your phantom community service should have been done at places that are not in the Yellow Pages of Oz.

The only skill you have, of course, is with a computer; but be careful not to let the company know that everything you did with your computer at college, even when you tried to have a little fun by moving those funds out of Citibank, has no value in the corporate world. At college, you used your computer to ask your parents for money, look for love on the Internet, and play mind-rotting games, three skills that are rarely called for at Pfizer or Ford.

Moreover, when writing your resumé, never take the advice of your friends, who will talk to you the way adults talk to each other about what the IRS will allow.

"You think the IRS will let me write off my money laundering?" an adult will ask a friend.

"Oh, of course," the friend will reply. "The IRS doesn't like dirty money."

And so, don't let a friend tell you to put on your resumé that you are pretender to the throne of Bulgaria or that you know how to make penicillin. Yes, your college room *was* full of mold, but it is wisest to stick to the lies that make a little sense.

Because your resumé will be of value to the company only in amusing the people who read it, you will have to be brilliant in the interview, and being brilliant is something you have always made it a habit to avoid. However, there are ways to fake almost anything, as you know from all the classes in which you almost read the books. A manual called *Job Interviews for Dummies* by Daniel T. Bobola has some helpful tips, even though a book for dummies may be above your level.

Find out where the interview is located.

Right. Going to the wrong address is invariably a setback for any interview.

Develop a couple of icebreaker sound bites, such as comments about a nice office, attractive color scheme, or interesting pictures.

Again I agree; in fact, you might use all three at once: "This is a nice office with an attractive color scheme and interesting pictures." No one has ever said this, so you'll score points for originality. Or you might take off into, "I like that photograph of Georgia O'Keeffe." The danger of such creativity is that the photo might be of the interviewer's wife. But no great damage will be done; you're in the wrong office anyway.

Prepare for tough specific questions like: If you could be an animal, what kind would you be?

If you're a young woman, here is your opportunity to score impressively.

"Man is *already* an animal," you can say. "*All* men are animals—except you, of course."

The biggest question you'll be asked is, Tell me about yourself. At last you have the essay question, the kind of bilge that got you through college, where you learned the valuable skill of how to speak at length on a subject while having no idea what you're talking about. At the interview, you'll need more than true or false answers and you'll be able to handle it.

Just remember that term paper you wrote called Myth, Symbol, and Punctuation in *The Hunchback of Notre Dame*, a paper to which you were able to give so much attention because you didn't waste time reading the book. Give the interviewer the kind of invention you gave your professor when you wrote:

> *The Hunchback of Notre Dame is* something else! Like, what I mean is this book is so allegorical that all its words really *mean* something else, if you know what I mean. For example, when the soldiers angrily march into the Cathedral of Notre Dame, it is clear that the author is talking about Army against Notre Dame. And when the priest speaks about the Big Ten, we know he means more than just the Commandments.

Perhaps you can make up for your interview and your resumé by taking some kind of company test. And perhaps, unlike one of my daughters, you happen to test well. Most companies, of course, will simply laugh off your resumé and then give you just an interview in which you can pretend to be somebody else; but once in a while, a company will give you an aptitude test and you will certainly be ready, particularly if it's multiple choice, because at college you developed the mental muscle to answer questions like these:

Conjunctivitis is:
    a. The compulsion to conjugate
    b. The excessive use of conjunctions
    c. An island near Greece

The period after the *Jurassic* is:
    a. The gestation
    b. Better than a comma
    c. All of the above

Martin Luther nailed his ninety-five points to the church door in Wittenberg because:
    a. He didn't have Scotch tape
    b. He couldn't afford a classified ad
    c. He was anxious to meet some Protestants

After you have honestly evaluated yourself, you will probably realize that the best thing going for you is nepotism. Take a good look at your family tree and see if you are related to anyone in the real world who might give you a job, either out of pity or because the company's policy calls for a token relative. Nepotism is a fine old American tradition: Blood is thicker than water and your relatives are thicker too.

"I'm going to tell my brother to hire you," your mother will say. "He owes me big for not turning him in to the IRS to collect a bounty to help with your tuition."

"He's the wrong relative, Mom," you'll reply. "I don't know anything about breeding dogs."

"What's there to know? They have sex, just without foreplay."

"I think I'd rather work for my cousin Clarence."

"You think you could pick up law easily? Well, that would be nice because you could help me sue your college for everything they forgot to teach you."

* * *

When you have a job interview with a relative, you can wear a bathrobe; but for interviews with strangers, you will need an adult's attire, something you never had at college, where the dress code was simply not to come to class with a visible pelvis. At college, if you were a guy, you thought that wearing a hat backward was turning the bill to the front; and you also thought that high fashion was baggy jeans with a bit of your underwear on display; you proudly walked around looking as though you were starting to undress. And you were the coolest if your lower spine was saying JOCKEY to the world.

Now, however, you are suddenly thrown into a world where grooming refers to more than horses, where it will be helpful to have a few suits, to have hair that doesn't block your view of the interviewer, and to have a nose that is free from costume jewelry.

I know one graduate who was fearing a callback for a second interview with a company.

"I only have one suit that my mother made me buy," he said. "Do you think they'll remember it?"

"Draw their attention away from it," I told him. "Don't wear a shirt."

"I was planning on that anyway. My shirt is in the laundry."

"You'll be showering?"

"Companies like that, right?"

"Except for strip mining companies, yes. Will you be showing any underwear?"

"My shorts won't stay above my belt; that's the problem with a suit. It's really hard to dress so fancy."

Although your liberal arts training, your lack of professional experience, and your unique intelligence might not get you any job except one as a trainee in a recycling plant, it *is* possible that you might be able to find a job through your social life. Unfortunately, as a new member of the real world, you may have to find a *Cliffs Notes* that tells you how to have a social life because that phrase has a different meaning now.

When you were at college, your parties were blends of wild dancing, cheap liquor, and music that has left you partially deaf. Some of the liquor, of course, wasn't cheap; but there was enough of it so that your college had proudly built its own rehab unit to turn students back into human beings. In the days when I went to college parties, students had to make their own slow way back to walking on two legs; but today a student guide who is giving a tour to high school seniors might say to them, "And in that building on the right, our students drop in to clean up their blood."

Parties in the real world, however, are often just conversation.

"Read any good books lately?" someone will say to you.

"Nothing has been assigned," you'll reply. "Say, what's your major?"

You probably have gone to the party to find someone you can marry because you are tired of hearing your mother say, "I want you to know that if you're a little unconventional and would rather date farm animals, it's perfectly all right with your father and me. We'll just change our names and move to Brazil."

* * *

At Temple, I was definitely someone who had the traditional male hormones. I remember a homecoming dance there when I began dancing with a vision named Laura and I was sweating so much that I was watering her wrist corsage, but I still was smooth enough to say, "What's your major?"

"World history," she said.

"Yeah, history. You mean stuff in the past. The past is cool."

There was no denying that I had an elegant way with words.

"The career you're headed for," I said. "You want to *do* anything with the past?"

"I want to be a travel agent," she said.

"Yeah, travel is cool," I replied. "Have you ever been to Asbury Park? And how about Manasquan in the moonlight."

"No, I mean the Taj Mahal and the Great Wall and the Dead Sea."

"They got a boardwalk on the Dead Sea?" I said. "They could sell a lot of saltwater taffy."

Sensing that my thoughts on travel weren't going anywhere, she said, "You play for some varsity, don't you, Bill?"

"Three, in fact: I'm a three-letter man."

D-U-D, I was starting to think, for I was sweating too much and moving her around as if I were trying to break the zone press.

"Do you run in the Penn Relays?" she said.

"Well, you don't stand still," I said. "That's a little college humor."

"If you say so."

"It comes easy to me."

"Like Falstaff."

"He at Temple too?"

In one way, at that college dance I was preparing for real life, where men are not as smart as women, or as some basset hounds. I realize I have already said this, but you're a college graduate, so I know your attention span. I'm surprised you've gotten this far.

"It's the Economy, Stupid" has been the dominant American slogan for the last few years, so let us see how college prepared you to succeed in this economy.

First, you learned calculus, which is very valuable if you want to be a calculus teacher. It is, however, of absolutely no use in the other six thousand professions. Luckily, you got a D plus, so you didn't make too great a mental or emotional investment.

Next, you learned how to have your parents send you extra money to buy the books the professors assigned that they just happened to write. Textbooks by professors always cost eighty-three dollars and are carefully written to go out of date every year. The books may be boring but the prices raise your pulse.

And third, although college didn't teach you how to balance a checkbook or to understand the wondrous ways in which a bank will be fleecing you, you did prepare to join the American economy by learning how to duck calls from Visa, Discover, and MasterCard.

What monetary memories you have! Remember the day you received your first unsolicited credit card, which you forgot to treat as junk mail? And the day you got your second, your third, and your fourth? It was thoughtful of the credit card companies to train you for a patriotic life by introducing you to something as American as baseball, Mom, and apple pie: debt. And now, just after graduation, you are an All-American adult: You owe $38,000 to Chase, Citibank, and the First Bank of Baghdad.

When you got this collection of credit cards, enough cards to have your own little booth at a credit card show, you didn't tell your parents, of course; you merely went out and bought things, for you remembered the philosopher who said that man lives only in the present. That philosopher ended in debtor's prison, but he still would have wanted you to have those seven cashmere sweaters.

Chapter Six

Should You Have Taken the *Conservative* Arts?

The real world is a reversal of college in so many ways: You no longer have Fridays off, you now go to a library to check out only books, and you no longer eat in a place where the food should be served to dolphins. Moreover, in the real world, your social life will be dramatically different because it will involve you with people whose approach on campus sent you ducking for cover.

You young women certainly remember the men you wouldn't dream of dating at school. Well, one of them will soon be your gynecologist, an approach to you he never dreamed of taking at school. And you young men certainly remember the women you wouldn't dream of dating at school? Well, one of them will soon be considering your application for a mortgage.

"Remember me from Dartmouth, Mr. Flintstone?"

"I believe I do, Ms. Prynne."

"You wouldn't talk to me, as I recall."

"I didn't dare; I was too intimidated by your loveliness. But how I admired you from afar!"

"You were a Deke, I believe."

"You *did* notice me."

"It was hard not to notice the Dekes, though I certainly tried. The animal house. Tell me, have you gone from the Deke house to a prison record of any kind?"

"No, most of us have successfully entered society."

"Now let me just check your application....We don't get too many in crayon. You're applying for this mortgage with Mrs. Flintstone?"

"Yes."

"You didn't meet her at Dartmouth, did you?"

"No, when I met Mrs. Flintstone, she was entertaining the troops at Fort Dix. Well, just outside Fort Dix, actually."

"And the two of you would like a ninety-thousand-dollar mortgage?"

"Yes, we found a nice place just off runway six at Newark Airport. A solid house; it shakes only for 747s."

Long before you have to consider a mortgage, you will have at least one job interview, which is the way that a company tries to get to know the real you, a process that you hope does not succeed. I'm aware that I have already talked about interviews, but I left something out, which undoubtedly is what you also will do.

In any job interview, it is important to speak

honestly, as long as you say what the interviewer wants to hear. Luckily, you had plenty of practice in producing that kind of stuff at college, where you played your professors' pet theories back to them in papers, essays on exams, and even casual campus chats:

"Hey, Professor Fontana! Man, I gotta tell ya, you changed my life when you said that Ponce de León was really looking for Philadelphia."

"Thank you, Mr. Cossey. Too few people appreciate the importance of Philadelphia to the early Spanish explorers."

And remember the history professor who felt that the lost tribe of Israel was the Seminoles? What an eloquent essay you wrote for her on Seminole synagogues. You even threw in a scholarly reference to kosher Kiowas.

At college, you also learned how to manufacture a fine brand of bologna about a popular modern theory called deconstructionism—and your work wasn't easy because no one knows what deconstruction *is*. All I know for sure is that it joined existentialism in the campus fog bank, giving students the chance to write a paper that would make *anything* grow: Deconstructing Existentialism. It was a paper that could have begun:

When they tore down Sartre's house...

Impressed, eh? You didn't think I knew what deconstructionism and existentialism were, did you? Well, I also know what nondenominationalism is. That's the belief that a church should take credit cards.

Whether or not a student learns what deconstructionism or existentialism is, college does give him or her a cosmic view, as I learned one day when one of my daughters gave me a much bigger picture than I wanted to see.

"I don't mean to bring up unpleasant things," I said to her, "but I was wondering if...I was wondering if you ever plan to look for...to look for..."

"The Loch Ness monster?" she said.

"Yes, that of course, but also a...well, I'll be delicate and spell it out: J-O-B."

"Oh, I know where Job is: right between Esther and Psalms. We learned all about the Bible at college."

"Good; we can pray together for you: Lord, let one of my children find a job before the end of the next millennium."

"Dad, it's no problem."

"Those *two words* again: *No problem.* That's what Pharaoh said when he was having a pleasant trip through the Red Sea and someone told him that a rather high tide was coming: 'No problem.' That's what the head of the Donner party said when someone told him they might be short a few box lunches: 'No problem.' And that's what the captain of the *Titanic* said when someone told him there had just been some kind of crunch: 'No problem.' No, actually he said, 'That was just the tip of the iceberg.'"

"Dad, you're getting much too emotional about employment. I'd be *happy* to look for a job, but right now I'm concentrating on *bigger* things."

"You mean like finding a way for your mother and me to get into your room without a machete?" I said.

"Dad, any time you want to come in, I'll be *happy* to cut out a path."

"You know, we've forgotten what color your rug is."

"But honestly, does seeing my floor really matter when the world is facing both global warming *and* a new ice age?"

"And you're working on both those problems from behind the slag heap?"

"*Somebody* has to."

"Is there any money in being a catastrophe consultant?"

"Money, money, money. Dad, you should be *proud* of me for forgetting about my own little problems and thinking instead about the future of mankind."

"But mankind doesn't shop at the Gap. Well, a little of it does, but—"

"Dad, I have so many bigger worries than the selfish one of making a living."

"You couldn't squeeze that one in, maybe between new viruses and a killer asteroid?"

"But *you* think about making a living, so isn't it silly for me to do exactly the same thing? I mean, it's *repetitious*."

"Well, I'm not an authority on the end of the world, but I do know that you can't worry about *both* global warming and a new ice age. They cancel each other out."

"Only if they come at the same *time*, silly."

"Of course. But couldn't you do your worrying while you have a job? Say, at your coffee break?"

"Dad, do you think I have so little concern about the human race that I'd make it a part-time thing? After all, why did you send me to college?"

"I'll ask your mother and let you know."

Many college graduates have occasional moments when they wonder why they studied what they did. Many, in fact, would like to start their college careers all over again and this time take courses that might have *some* connection to *something*. Well, a great number of colleges now realize that a fine education doesn't lead anywhere; and so, to make college more appealing to people who may have skipped high school, these schools have been moving away from the frill courses (like history, philosophy, and learning to write compete sentences) and giving students a chance to take the kind of courses offered by a Pittsburgh YMCA.

For example, in early 1999 at Penn State University, the number of classes in ballroom dancing was increased from eight to forty-eight; and across the entire country, from Bates to Arizona State, ballroom dancing has become a popular elective.

"What's your major at college?" an adult today will foolishly say to a young student.

"I'm majoring in the macarena," she will reply, "with a minor in Inca fertility rites. For my senior thesis, I'm going to Peru to reproduce. On a volcano. My boyfriend is coming with me. He's a Madonna Fellow at Yale."

The State University of New York is now offering a course called Revolting Behavior. When I first heard about the course, I thought it was a study of a high school lunchroom; but then I learned it was about women's sexual freedom. Well, Revolting Behavior is a good example of the way that the college curriculum is both evolving and dissolving. In fact, several colleges have actually decided that teaching grammar is wrong because it offends all the students who want to feel good about being illiterate.

My grandchildren will have schedules that will prepare them for life with courses like these:

AN INTRODUCTION TO
CRAZY EIGHTS
Three credits. Professor David "Doc" Morgan
PREREQUISITE: *Go Fish 1-2*

A survey of the playing of crazy eights since Roman times, with particular emphasis on how the game has evolved from crazy threes. Why the Moors were unhappy with crazy sevens. Why the Crusaders played casino instead.

Extra credit for a paper discussing whether the politically incorrect name of the game should now be changed to dysfunctional eights out of respect to both Crazy Horse and all the non–Native Americans who are definitely strange.

One field trip to Atlantic City.

COMMUNICATIONS 101: USE OF THE TELEPHONE
Three credits. Professor Judy Danzig

Students will learn how to both place and receive calls and then move on to an inquiry into the meaning of a busy signal. No previous telephone experience is required. Advance work in speed dialing is optional, as is advance work in learning how to take a cell phone call during a concert by a string quartet.

COMMUNICATIONS 102: CALLER ID
Three credits. Professor Max Heinz
PREREQUISITE: *A general knowledge of numbers*

Students will learn how to read caller ID and decide if they want to return the call.

Advance work in not returning calls is available for students planning to enter show business.

THE MALTED MILK

Three credits. Professor Lori Morath
PREREQUISITE: *The Milk Shake*

A study of the history of the malted milk from its foamy beginnings until its corruption at the first Dairy Queen. An analysis of the effect of the malted milk on the environment from the use of Cool Whip. And an attempt to answer the timeless question: Does a chocolate malted exist if it is made with vanilla ice cream?

THEORY AND PRACTICE OF BEACH VOLLEYBALL

Three credits. Professor "Pam"
PREREQUISITE: *Tanning 1-2*

A comprehensive look at the playing of beach volleyball throughout history. An attempt to answer the question: How many IQ points are lost from a year of beach volleyball? Extra credit for discovering why "Dover Beach" has no reference to volleyball.

PRINCIPLES AND PRACTICES OF SPACKLING

Three credits. Professor Peter Levin

PREREQUISITE: *Some previous experience with glue besides sniffing it*

Students will decide if they would rather work on cracks or holes. There will also be study of the great spacklers, like Michelangelo and Bob Villas.

GENDER: FACT OR FICTION?

Three credits. Professor Ginger Gothard

PREREQUISITE: *Some familiarity with men and women*

The course will attempt to answer these questions: Are the differences between men and women inborn, learned, or imagined? Since a woman has a better sense of smell than a man, is it correct to say that she smells better? And why do females talk and shop so much earlier than males, and why would only a man ask questions like these? Moreover, why is typical male behavior both leaving up the toilet seat and going to war?

Because these explorations of gender are too substantial for a modern course, attendance at class is optional.

The important thing to remember is that not a single one of these new courses *or* the more traditional ones will prepare you for entering the job market, though a fish market might have a place for you.

"I majored in government and minored in African American studies," one young man said to me. "What kind of job does *that* lead to?"

"You could be a poll-watcher in Nairobi," I told him.

"Is there any money in that?"

"It's an entry-level position."

Such other new courses as A History of Heartburn and The Theory and Practice of Taking Out Trash may seem a bit short on scholarship, but they are probably better preparation for life than a study of the Hundred Years' War. Even the people who *fought* the Hundred Years' War stopped paying attention around the fortieth year, and the attention span is a lot shorter now.

And so, to prepare a student for a life in which he will spend most of his time web and channel surfing, a college has to cater to this new attention span with courses in the history of makeup, vacuuming, hip-hop, and lunch. Most students today don't even learn the alma mater because you can't dance to it.

These new courses in College Lite are so appealing that many students are inspired to turn their fear of the real world into a return to college, where they can audit undergraduate courses without a fee, or move onward and upward to graduate school, where they embrace knowledge that is even more worthless than what they learned at college.

Of all the ways to avoid real life, from joining a religious order to trying to find the Abominable Snowman, none has been more popular than going to graduate school. Millions of college graduates take a quick look at the outside and then, like parolees who miss the penal womb, they go right back inside the walls. Some graduate courses do lead to such things as accounting, dentistry, and law, all of which from time to time are of use to society; but dozens of other courses lead directly to a degree that should be called Master of Nothing in Particular.

Academic bums is what they are called, but that isn't fair. They make a profession out of hiding in graduate school.

Graduate school is appealing not just as a sanctuary but because, like College Lite, it calls for a minimal use of English; and if you finally find the courage to leave the campus and accidentally find a job, you still will not be required to speak anything that makes sense.

When you see my face in libraries on a poster that says READ, you know that I've been a lover of that passing fad, literacy. I've spent many years encouraging young people to go to books instead of the mall. However, I am afraid that one day soon, young people won't be reading much more than BANANA REPUBLIC

Did he mean that Rice was near a university? All we know for sure is that his school is now Minute Rice. And we know that some future application to Duke will begin, "I would like to go, like, to Dook due to I love a school that always makes the Final Fore."

How much longer will kids be able to read my library poster? Do you think it will ever say REED?

All this dumbing down, of course, does prepare the graduate for a world where one New York sportswriter said, "*Charles Barkley* likes to flaunt the rules." He was saying that Barkley likes to brandish the rules to show how proud he is of them.

The correct word is *flout*. Or is it *grout*? Pretty soon, most males may *think* it's grout because fewer and fewer of them are even going to college. According to *U.S. News & World Report*, a magazine that says almost as much about our world as *Mad*, 60 percent of college students are now female because more men are "going directly from high school into such jobs as air conditioner maintenance instead of four years of *Beowulf* and college loans."

and EXIT. And the incredible thing is that this dumbing down is being led by our *colleges*, where cell phones and beepers are sounding instead of an alarm.

Remember my saying that several colleges have stopped teaching grammar because it annoys students who enjoy being illiterate? Well, one of those schools is Duke and you won't believe this story. But you know that, unlike my children, I never lie.

Last year, a friend of mine took his daughter, a high school senior, to Duke, where the two of them heard an assistant dean of admissions say, "When you come to Duke, you won't have to worry about spelling or grammar. We want to know your feelings; we really don't care how you write."

"That's great," my friend's daughter said to him. "My papers will be easier to write if I don't have to use grammar; that always slows me down."

"And maybe verbs are optional too," he replied.

Meanwhile, last fall in a TV promotion for his school during the halftime of a football game, one college senior said, "Rice is really well situated toward learning."

In the college of tomorrow, there may be only token males, those who couldn't get into air conditioner maintenance schools, those who think that freon is one of Beowulf's trolls.

"Well, my boy," the father of tomorrow's graduate will say, "now that you know all about *Beowulf*, maybe you could get a job that has something to do with tending sheep. It's too late to become a Maytag man."

Chapter Seven

No More
Pre-Caressing
Agreements

I have to keep coming back to the subject of social life because it can be quite challenging and because we don't seem to be getting anywhere with a job for you. Sometime after you graduate, you may want to have a social life that does more for your glands than dinner with your mother; but it won't be easy because college has given you four years of finding other sexes within a few feet of your room.

There is, of course, one way to date without leaving your home: with your PC. In fact, you'll be spending much of your postgraduate life online, where you'll be searching for jobs, bargains, scandals, space aliens, and people of a different sex.

I don't know how to use a computer; I'm still trying to learn a washing machine. To me, a hard drive is the Long Island Expressway; but the computer is where *you* will be living and maybe finding someone to help you make your way through the scary postgraduate world, particularly if he or she has money. Even if you can't find a job or an apartment, you might be able to use cyberspace to find someone to share your idleness. More than a million people are already lying about themselves online and twenty thousand new ones come online every week. Your college essays on the books you almost read prepared you not only for writing your resumé but also for the style of your online personal:

> *I may live in Schenectady, but I look like Helen of Troy. Eventually I'd like to be either a masseuse or*

*a neurosurgeon; I want to keep my options open.
Maybe one of my options is you. My grade point
average was 4.0, my temperature is 98.6, and I'm
as loyal as a basset hound and just as frisky.*

You young men who feel that college hasn't prepared you to leave the house might want to look for
romance with poetic words like these:

*"Someday My Prince Will Come" just happens to
refer to me, so don't you be bashful, dopey, or
sleepy. Answer me and get to know someone who
is handsome, witty, charming, athletic, modest,
and devoted to world peace, mental health, and
firmer abs. I have a complete set of genes, I am
crazy about low interest rates, and I have always
felt that women are more than just irrational men.
I would like to share these beliefs with you, especially if you have a car.*

If online dating leads you only to people who
are even stranger than you, then you have to jump-

start your social life by doing something unheard of at college: You have to leave the house. Not only leave it but actually travel away from your street, even though you may have to take out a loan to buy some bus tokens.

At college, you had an endless supply of people of another sex, but you always saw them at their worst, in baggy clothes and badly groomed; even the men looked like this. Now, however, you have to go hunting and the game preserve is huge. You have to look for a very rare species called "those who will understand you."

It is especially important to leave the house if you are still living at home. First of all, how many attractive single people can you find at home? An occasional UPS man, perhaps; they do look cute in those shorts, and the FedEx women are even more fetching. Yes, if enough people ship things to your house, you may find the delivery person of your dreams; but the house is not the ideal place for a relationship deeper than signing a receipt. You do not want a scene like this:

YOUR MOTHER: *(calling from just outside the living room)* Roger, is there someone out there on the couch with you?

ROGER: Just a new friend, Mom. I'm accepting something.

YOUR MOTHER: Roger, does the friend happen to be the same sex as you?

ROGER: No, a different one, Mom. I'm celebrating diversity.

YOUR MOTHER: Well, remember my rule: No more reproducing in the house. Your father and I did the last of it and frankly it could have turned out better.

Yes, dating now demands that you look for people outside the house. The postgraduate woman does not want a young man to make an evening of coming to her house to sink into the couch and sprinkle crumbs while watching TV. That kind of evening was fine back at school, where both of them were brought together by a common love of avoiding the work; but now the young man has to *take* her somewhere. The problem, of course, is that the young man has just about enough money to take her to court.

"An evening of dinner, theater, and dancing is so *ordinary*," he says to her. "Instead, let's catch the early show at magistrate's court, eat a couple of soft pretzels, and then go down to the Amtrak yard to watch some coupling. I think coupling is wonderful, don't you?"

"Sam, we're not at college anymore," she replies. "People on dates out here actually do something that has the potential to be entertaining."

"Well, we could go to your place."

"And play Scrabble with my roommates?"

"I'd take you back to *my* place, but my mother is shampooing the rugs. You see, Katie, right now I have what the Federal Reserve would call a negative cash flow."

"Well, that's okay. As long as you're not broke."

In one way, however, dating will now be easier because you're free from the campus sex police, who were ready to charge you with sexual harassment if you put your hand on any woman besides one who had asked you for help in crossing the street. At some schools, there are now even *manuals* for sexual exploration that tell the men the permissions they need before they can start the rake's progress. Of course, if I know these young men, they will probably just jump to the *Cliffs Notes* for the manuals and read:

> *The left breast. Get clearance.*
> *The right breast. See left.*

No matter how good college was, you have to be happy that you are no longer at a place where a scene like this is the essence of romance:

THE PLACE: *A leafy college campus lane.*

THE TIME: *Nine o'clock on an evening in early May. In the air is the scent of apple blossom and the feeling of final tuition payments due.*

A male and female student are strolling along, three feet apart.

MALE: *(calling to the female)* I'm really glad you agreed to go out with me, Louise.

FEMALE: *(calling back to him)* Well, I heard violins when you filled out the pre-foreplay form.

MALE: *(moving slightly closer to her)* You…you look so lovely in the moonlight.

FEMALE: George—

MALE: My name is Max.

FEMALE: Max, I don't want you to have a record, so I'll pretend you didn't say that without permission. Do I have to quote the Supreme Court on *Ruddy v. Weinstock and Kansas State?*

MALE: Sorry. Okay, Simon says: May I look at your face?

FEMALE: Yes you may, but please don't get any ideas.

MALE: The last thing I have at college is ideas.

FEMALE: I certainly don't want you thinking I'm a different gender or anything.

MALE: Of course not; gender is in the eye of the

beholder. One of yours is blue, you know. I can tell from way over here.

FEMALE: Are you trying for a mug shot, Max? I have a lot of friends at nine-one-one.

MALE: Sorry, that's just the testosterone talking. Look, I know I forgot the form, but why don't we sit a while on this bench and enjoy the soft spring evening.

FEMALE: Well…all right, but I don't want you to wonder if I'm ovulating.

MALE: That's the *last* thing I'd suspect a girl like you of doing!

FEMALE: Frankly, it's a habit I'm trying to break; and it wouldn't be a bad idea if you got rid of all that testosterone too.

MALE: Yes, I know the behavior it caused in Attila the Hun and John F. Kennedy.

FEMALE: I try not to think about either of them.

(For a few moments, they sit quietly on a bench. Max sneaks a look at the moon while Louise snuggles

up to her copy of The Illinois Criminal Code.)

MALE: Louise, I simply can't help it! Let's *forget* the entire sweep of English common law and let me hold your hand? I'll start with whichever one is less erogenous.

FEMALE: My whole *hand*? Out of the question; I'm saving that for my husband. But...well, a couple of knuckles might be okay.

MALE: Oh, be still my heart! How those crackling little connections intoxicate me!

FEMALE: Do you happen to have a permission slip for any upper extremity?

MALE: The harassment office was out of them; it had only the toes. But Justice Brandeis said that an oral contract would cover it.

FEMALE: Max, do you really think I would be involved in anything *oral*? That's for Sodom and Gomorrah.

MALE: Sodom and Gomorrah? Are they in the Big Ten?

Chapter Eight

Is a Semiconductor Half of André Previn?

One basic problem that confronts most college

graduates, even if they have jobs, is the bewildering

world of American finance.

"I just got a job," one graduate told me, "and a

big chunk of every check I get goes to FICA. What's

that, a tree? Is that money going to save the rain

forest."

"No," I told him, "that's for Social Security. That's

so you can retire someday and spend many rewarding hours at the dog track."

"Is there any way for me to get them to stop making that deduction?"

"Yes, of course there is. You can become a citizen of Guatemala."

"But this Social Security scam…a professor told me that Social Security will be bankrupt by the time I'm supposed to get it."

"Well," I said, "the government has a lot of bombing to do. And they also insist on paying congressmen."

"So my paying Social Security, it's like playing a broken slot machine."

"Actually, your odds at a broken slot machine are a little better. When you retire, the government will just have to owe it to you. Owing money is a very American thing."

"You mean like the money I owe Sallie Mae?"

"How much did she lend you?"

"No, Sallie Mae makes student loans."

"Well, I think it's great that women now can be

loan sharks too. It takes real dedication for them to learn how to break your legs."

"Sallie Mae is a *bank*."

"You've taught me something about the economy. I wish I could teach you graduates how to understand it, but nobody really does, especially now that the twenty dollar bill is so ugly. For instance, a few months ago, the government announced that unemployment was down but layoffs were up."

"How is that possible?" he said.

"I think it means there's less unemployment among people who are out of work."

"Yes, FICA is definitely a tree. Or a way to cover your floor."

Shortly after graduation, my daughter said, "I never knew that cereal cost so much."

"Yes, it's not the flakes you eat," I said, "it's the flakes who pay millions of dollars for endorsements by athletes who wouldn't go *near* the cereal. Honey, you're seeing what the real world is like. Want to think about graduate school?"

Ironically, my daughter had just come from a campus where most of the job recruiting for seniors had been by brokerage houses, banks, and other businesses whose only product was money. There were no recruiters from Lincoln Center or the Museum of Modern Art because, as Calvin Coolidge said, "The business of America is business." Don't worry if you were a psychology major and never heard of Calvin Coolidge. During his presidency, most people never heard of him either.

At any rate, at campuses all over what is still Coolidge country, scenes like this one are being played:

BANK RECRUITER: I'd like to interest you in joining us. Tell me, would it bother you to get huge annual bonuses when so many people are below the poverty line?

SENIOR: One of those people is me. Could I have an advance?

BANK RECRUITER: You sound like a young man with a feel for finance.

SENIOR: No load…no load…I've *seen* it on trucks.

BANK RECRUITER: That's good enough. Tell me, would you have any qualms about foreclosing on a house? I mean, you're no *Grapes of Wrath* wimp, are you?

SENIOR: No, I believe in the American way. Everyone has the right to be put out on the street.

BANK RECRUITER: Yes, John D. Rockefeller taught us that. He was a deeply religious man.

SENIOR: There *is* one more thing I'd like to know about working at your bank. Will I have a chance to take a nap?

And now, we have come at last to the most difficult part of the transition from the fantasy life of the campus to the reality of the world, for now the graduate has to try a revolutionary way of sleeping: at night. People coming from college are often unaware of the custom of sleeping at night that is popular in many states. At college, especially just before exams, it is common to have an "all-nighter," which is a heroic attempt to learn

SENIOR: I'm also nuts about money. Would that work for you people?

BANK RECRUITER: Are you an economics major?

SENIOR: Not exactly. I've been majoring in Mayan affairs. Ask me anything about the barter system.

BANK RECRUITER: Well, perhaps you could develop some Mayan customers; diversity is very important at our bank. Why, just this month, I foreclosed on a stuttering gypsy and a bulimic Methodist.

SENIOR: I hear you lend money only to people who don't need it.

BANK RECRUITER: Those are the happiest loans, yes. Lending money to poor people can lead to problems. However, if you want to work with Mayan customers, we'd certainly let you encourage the building of new pyramids, at twelve percent.

SENIOR: What would my starting salary be?

BANK RECRUITER: We can start you at forty thousand dollars. Fifty if you know what a no-load fund is.

the entire course in seven hours. This attempt can work if the course is naming the planets or the parts of the face, but the history of Greece may take longer.

I remember one all-nighter at Temple when my roommate and I were trying to learn the history of Greece for a morning exam. It was exhilarating to plunge into new material. By seven A.M., we had gotten up to the sixth century.

"Did anything happen after that?" I said to my roommate.

"Nothing really big," he replied. "In Greece, they did all the big stuff early. After that, they just invented souvlaki."

At college, sleep was an elective for you. In the real world, however, someone who stays up all night and then goes to work is liable to end up facedown in the office shredder, nose-to-nose with all the information that should have gone to the FBI. Postgraduate life, in fact, is a kind of endless jet lag in which the graduate never quite manages to make up for the amount of sleep that he lost at college.

"My greatest motivation right now," one graduate told me, "is to enter a program for taking naps. I want to develop my skill at falling asleep not only when people like you are talking but also at meaningful times during the day."

"Yes," I told her, "I can understand how hard it is to motivate yourself for other things now."

"Exactly. There's no exam coming up and no paper due. In fact, *nothing* is due and I'm not sure I can handle that. Tell me, are there any jobs that give spot quizzes?"

If there *is* a dream job for you, one that gives spot quizzes and Fridays off and starts at ten A.M. and doesn't believe in FICA, you still may not get it if you come from college stapled and stamped—in other words, with rings and pins and tattoos all over your body. At American colleges today, many students are turning their bodies into moving pop art; they have more holes in their head than they did when I went to school and many of those heads are also changing color. A CBS report recently said that American children as young as nine are now dyeing their hair. But when I was a boy, a kid called Red held on to that name and never had to be renamed Fuchsia.

Many college students today are works in progress. On one visit to Howard, I saw a young woman with five rings in her earlobe. I wondered if she was making a dramatic fashion statement or if she worked for the Olympics. Another student had one ring in his nose and one in his ear. I wondered if the next jewelry would be for his tonsils, perhaps a gift from his mother.

"Here's a little bauble for you, son. I think it would look lovely down your throat."

If you do go to a job interview—your parents want me to keep reminding you that there is such a thing—and you go there looking like a bull that has been involved with a picador, there are a few things to remember. First of all, make sure that all your rings are shined; a tarnished ring gives a poor impression. Next, make sure that there is no ring connecting your upper lip to your lower. You want to be able to open your mouth, in case you think of anything to say. And also wear rings that are in good taste: plain little bands and not rhinestones. You certainly don't want to call attention to yourself.

Your tattoos, of course, will be concealed, unless you happen to be a young woman in a sleeveless summer dress. If you are, then be ready to explain to the interviewer why your right shoulder has a rendering of Lizzie Borden above the words *Remember Mother*.

"I have a profound feeling for both the family and American history," you might say. "I have my father on my chest and the Battle of Midway on my behind. But don't worry: I still have room for the company logo, maybe under one of my arms."

With nine-year-olds as role models, many college students are also wearing their hair in colors for which there are no genes. If *you* happen to have a head that's an alternate color, one that nature didn't think of, and you are about to be interviewed for a job, it will be important to wear clothes that match.

"Do you think this dress goes with my hair?" a

young female graduate asked a woman I know just before an interview.

"Well, not quite," my friend replied. "I'm afraid that dress doesn't really work with purple. You either need a yellow dress or you have to make your hair green."

"*Green*?" said the young woman. "That's *crazy*."

"I know."

"I *had* my hair green for part of my senior year and it was a real mistake."

"I imagine it would be."

"It was such a *cliché*."

"You mean other people at Iowa State had green hair?"

"I mean, who *didn't*? By the way, I like *your* hair. What formula is that?"

"It's called natural."

"No kidding. Sort of a salute to the olden days."

"Right. It actually has a DNA."

"Maybe someday I'll try natural too. Where do you buy it?"

To Duck the Bright Tomorrow

Once again, congratulations!

In the weeks it has taken you to read this far, I presume you are still dedicated to being a late bloomer, in spite of the unfortunate names that your loved ones are giving you. I presume you still know how unhappy the Puritans were with all that work. In fact, at least one of them was heard to say, "Isn't there some *other* ethic around?"

Well, stay with your dream and don't be concerned when your mother asks a few times a day, "What *now*?" and "Have you thought about the merchant marines?" and "Why are your pupils dilated?" You have got to leave yourself open for all the possibilities that have nothing to *do* with making enough money to stay alive. In a dog-eat-dog world, there is certainly room for a turtle like you, creeping along and occasionally retracting your head.

You do not have to be led astray by all the people who are doing useful and productive things. Remember that Thoreau said, "If a man does not keep pace with his companions, perhaps it is because he hears a different drummer." Well, yours plays with Smashing Pumpkins and for you every day can be Halloween.

Thoreau was even goofier than you and maybe you will decide to follow his example. Maybe you'll go far from the competitive world and all your creditors and become a forest ranger. A liberal arts education certainly prepares you to pick up the phone and say, "Fire! I think it's Wyoming."

Or, instead of putting on your best nose ring

and joining the establishment, maybe you'll reject all the coldness of business and volunteer at a sperm bank. Or maybe you'll be what *Newsweek* recently called the worker-in-waiting, "who has figured out that college should be more than four years of career training." Well, the dean and I already have given you an even more important thought: College is also *less* than four years of career training.

Higher education and postgraduate life have been changing dramatically and your way of life suddenly makes more sense than the dean ever knew when he asked you if you really wanted to major in probation. In fact, a fitting alma mater for an American college in the new millennium would be:

O Quarry State, O Quarry State,
What fools we were to graduate!
For as we wander far and near,
We don't know if we're there or here.
Thy walls of stone, thy minds of moss
Are what we'll miss—and sleep, of course.

No matter how long you may be wandering in the wilderness of real life, no matter how sincerely you may be looking for a place to lie down, you did go to college and that was *good*, for you now are smart enough to know how to duck the bright tomorrow. And if nothing ever turns up with a four-day week, a three-hour lunch, and a holiday for Count Basie's birthday, you still might be able to make a few dollars on *Jeopardy*. Just remember that Billy *Strayhorn* wrote "Take the 'A' Train," that footballs aren't made of pigskin, and that it was Fat Albert and not Plato who said, "Just because you're grown up don't mean you have to be an adult."